RACING SPORTS

INDYCAR RACING

BY ELIZABETH HOBBS VOSS

WWW.APEXEDITIONS.COM

Apex is distributed by North Star Editions:
sales@northstareditions.com | 888-417-0195

Produced for Apex by Red Line Editorial.

Photographs ©: Tom E. Puskar/AP Images, cover; Phil Long/AP Images, 1, 16–17; Brian Spurlock/Icon Sportswire/AP Images, 4–5, 20–21; Dan Sanger/Icon Sportswire/AP Images, 6–7; Shutterstock Images, 8, 19, 24–25; Michael Conroy/AP Images, 9; AP Images, 10–11, 12–13; Darron Cummings/AP Images, 14–15; David Boe/AP Images, 18; Thurman James/Cal Sport Media/ZUMA Wire/AP Images, 22–23, 29; Greg Huey/AP Images, 26

Library of Congress Control Number: 2022923628

ISBN
978-1-63738-537-1 (hardcover)
978-1-63738-591-3 (paperback)
978-1-63738-697-2 (ebook pdf)
978-1-63738-645-3 (hosted ebook)

Printed in the United States of America
Mankato, MN
082023

NOTE TO PARENTS AND EDUCATORS

Apex books are designed to build literacy skills in striving readers. Exciting, high-interest content attracts and holds readers' attention. The text is carefully leveled to allow students to achieve success quickly. Additional features, such as bolded glossary words for difficult terms, help build comprehension.

TABLE OF CONTENTS

CHAPTER 1

START YOUR ENGINES

The Indianapolis 500 is about to start. Thirty-three drivers wait in the **starting grid**. They watch for the green flag.

The driver in the best starting spot is called the pole sitter.

The flag waves, and the race begins. Drivers zoom down the track. They speed around and around for 200 laps.

FAST FACT

The Indianapolis 500 is the most famous IndyCar race. It is 500 miles (805 km) long.

The track for the Indianapolis 500 is 2.5 miles (4 km) long.

IndyCars can go more than 230 miles per hour (370 km/h).

The drivers turn the final corner. It's a close race. But one car pulls ahead. It crosses the finish line, and the huge crowd cheers.

MANY TRADITIONS

The Indianapolis 500 has many **traditions**. It always takes place on Memorial Day weekend. Fans sing "Back Home Again in Indiana." And the winner gets a bottle of milk.

Helio Castroneves holds up his bottle of milk after winning the Indianapolis 500 in 2001.

CHAPTER 2

INDYCAR HISTORY

IndyCar racing is one of the oldest kinds of car racing. The first race happened in 1909. Six cars made three laps around a track.

The first IndyCars could only go about 56 miles per hour (90 km/h).

In 1911, the first Indianapolis 500 was held. Many people watched. IndyCar racing became popular. Drivers raced on tracks throughout the United States.

The Indianapolis Motor Speedway is nicknamed the Brickyard. It used to be paved in bricks.

FAST FACT

Early IndyCar tracks were often made of wood or dirt.

In the 1990s, IndyCar racing split into two **leagues**. Fewer people watched races. But the groups came back together in 2008. They formed the new, modern version of IndyCar racing.

WOMEN RACING

Most IndyCar drivers are men. But women race IndyCars, too. In 1977, Janet Guthrie became the first woman to race in the Indianapolis 500.

CHAPTER 3

RULES AND TRACKS

There are 22 races in the IndyCar **series** each year. Each event begins with **qualifying** rounds. The fastest drivers move on to the main race.

Drivers with top speeds in qualifying rounds get better positions in the main race.

Drivers earn points for their place in each race. At the end of the series, the driver with the most points wins the championship.

Drivers get the most points for finishing first, second, or third. They can also get points for leading some laps.

A. J. Foyt raced for several decades. He won seven IndyCar championships.

FAST FACT

A. J. Foyt won the most IndyCar championships. He also had the most wins in one season.

IndyCar races happen on different kinds of tracks. Speedways are short ovals. Road courses are longer. Each has a different shape. Street circuits run through cities.

SENDING MESSAGES

IndyCar racing uses nine flags. Each flag gives drivers a message. The green flag means "go." A checkered flag signals the end of the race.

The Honda Indy Toronto race uses a street circuit.

CHAPTER 4

CARS AND EQUIPMENT

IndyCars have open **cockpits** and just one seat. They are open-wheel cars. That means the wheels are on the outside.

IndyCars can cost more than $3 million to build and race.

IndyCars are lighter than some other types of race cars. But they have strong engines that help them go fast.

It takes a lot of training to be part of a pit crew.

PIT STOPS

IndyCars need to be fixed during races. So, drivers make fast **pit stops**. The crew changes tires and adds fuel. All the fixes can happen in just seven seconds.

FUZZY'S
VODKA
Firestone
20

IndyCar racing can be dangerous. So, drivers wear strong helmets and clothes that can't catch fire. **Barriers** along racetrack walls also protect drivers if they crash.

FAST FACT

In 2020, safety screens were added to the cockpits of IndyCars.

Because of the high speeds and open cockpits, crashes in IndyCar racing can be deadly.

COMPREHENSION QUESTIONS

Write your answers on a separate piece of paper.

1. Write a few sentences that explain the main ideas of Chapter 3.
2. Do you think IndyCar racing is too dangerous? Why or why not?
3. What kind of IndyCar tracks are shaped like ovals?
   - A. road courses
   - B. street circuits
   - C. speedways
4. How could adding safety screens to IndyCar cockpits protect drivers?
   - A. The screens could make the cars lighter.
   - B. The screens could keep things from hitting drivers' heads.
   - C. The screens could block drivers' views.

5. What does **modern** mean in this book?

But the groups came back together in 2008. They formed the new, ***modern*** *version of IndyCar racing.*

A. used very long ago
B. no longer used
C. being used today

6. What does **signals** mean in this book?

The green flag means "go." A checkered flag ***signals*** *the end of the race.*

A. stops a car
B. sends a message
C. takes a picture

Answer key on page 32.

GLOSSARY

barriers

Walls of foam and steel that act as cushions in crashes.

cockpits

The parts of race cars where the drivers sit.

leagues

Groups of drivers or teams that compete against one another.

pit stops

Times when race cars stop to get fuel or repairs.

qualifying

Types of earlier races used to pick where drivers will start in later races.

series

The set of IndyCar races that take place around the world each year.

starting grid

An area of the track where drivers line up to begin the race.

traditions

Beliefs or ways of doing things that have existed for a long time.

TO LEARN MORE

BOOKS

Adamson, Thomas K. *Indy Cars*. Minneapolis: Bellwether Media, 2019.

Braulick, Carrie A. *Indy Cars*. North Mankato, MN: Capstone Press, 2019.

Fishman, Jon M. *Cool Indy Cars*. Minneapolis: Lerner Publications, 2019.

ONLINE RESOURCES

Visit **www.apexeditions.com** to find links and resources related to this title.

ABOUT THE AUTHOR

Elizabeth Hobbs Voss is a children's writer and journalist. She enjoys writing books that entertain and educate young people. She is the author of several children's books. She lives in New York City with her husband, Todd.

INDEX

ANSWER KEY:

1. Answers will vary; 2. Answers will vary; 3. C; 4. B; 5. B; 6. C